"Yes, he seems to do little but wander around the town each day.

I wonder who sends him all those letters …"

Original Korean text by Yu-ri Kim
Illustrations by Jeong-yeon Lim
Korean edition © Aram Publishing

This English edition published by big & SMALL in 2016
by arrangement with Aram Publishing
English text edited by Scott Forbes
English edition © big & SMALL 2016

Distributed in the United States and Canada by
Lerner Publishing Group, Inc.
241 First Avenue North
Minneapolis, MN 55401 U.S.A.
www.lernerbooks.com

ISBN: 978-1-925249-10-1

Printed in Korea

The Friendly Postman

THE ART OF VAN GOGH

Written by Yu-ri Kim

Illustrated by Jeong-yeon Lim

Edited by Scott Forbes

Postman Roulin was delivering the mail.
"How is your flu?" asked a neighbor.
"Much better, thank you."
"Mr. Roulin, do we have any mail?"
"Not today, madam. Maybe next time!"

He took the last letter out of his mailbag.
"Phew, just one more delivery to do,"
he said to himself.

Postman Roulin knocked on
the door of a yellow house.
Nobody answered.
He knocked again, but all was quiet.
"Letter for you!" shouted Mr. Roulin.
The door creaked open, just a little bit.

A hand appeared through the gap. Peering inside, Mr. Roulin could see green eyes and a shock of red hair.

"You must be new to the town," he said to the man.

Mr. Roulin smiled. But the man simply snatched the letter and slammed the door shut.

Mr. Roulin was shocked.

Self-portrait (1889), Musée d'Orsay, Paris, France

11

Every day after that, another letter arrived
for the man in the yellow house.
And each day Mr. Roulin went there to deliver it.
But every time the man would only snatch the
letter from his hand and slam the door shut.

Mr. Roulin noticed that the person who sent
the letters to the man was called Theo.
"He seems to write almost every day," he said
to himself. "He's a loyal friend."

13

Mr. Roulin met a friend at a café for dinner.
"Hey, Joseph," said his friend. "Don't you think
that man in the yellow house is strange? He just
wanders around town all day or sits here and drinks."
"Well … I don't know," replied Mr. Roulin.

Soon, other people started gossiping about the man.
Mr. Roulin wanted
to find out more
about him.

Then the letters for the man stopped arriving.
"I wonder what's going on," thought
Mr. Roulin.

He kept looking for a letter
from Theo. But none came.
"That poor man must be wondering what
has happened," thought Mr. Roulin.
Every day he passed the yellow house,
he looked to see if the man was there.

A month went by. Still no letters came for the man.
Mr. Roulin gradually forgot about him.
Then, one day, he saw a letter with the name
Theo on it. "He'll be very happy
            when I take this to him," thought Mr. Roulin.

Bureau de Poste

17

18

When Mr. Roulin knocked, the man came to the door.

"Letter for you!" said Mr. Roulin.

"Thank you … thank you so much," replied the man quietly.

And, for the first time, he smiled at Mr. Roulin.

"He seems so nice," thought Mr. Roulin, as he looked at the man.

"Why would anyone think he is strange?"

That night, Mr. Roulin was coming
home late after delivering letters
to a neighboring town.
As he was passing a field of yellow wheat,
someone staggered out onto the road.

Mr. Roulin got a bit of a fright.
"Are you alright?" he said.
It was the man from the yellow house.
He had yellow paint all over his hands.

Mr. Roulin helped the man home
and got him to lie down on his bed.
He was clearly confused. He kept calling
out "Theo," while groaning as if in pain.
Mr. Roulin stayed by his side
until he calmed down.

The next evening at supper, Mrs. Roulin
started talking about the man.
"You know that man in the yellow house?
I hear he's crazy.

They say that every night he
goes wandering in the fields."

"If you don't know for sure,
you shouldn't talk ill of him,"
said Mr. Roulin, suddenly angry.

25

Mr. Roulin was worried about
the man. So the next day
he went to the yellow house
early in the morning.

He noticed the door was open a little.
Carefully, he crept inside.
And there he got a huge surprise.
Sitting on an easel was a painting
of him — Mr. Roulin!
Next to it was a letter, which
Mr. Roulin picked up and read.

Dear Mr. Roulin,

I waited for you every day.
The letters you brought were from my brother.
People find me strange, but my brother
has always understood and helped me.

Like my brother, you were nice to me.
Unfortunately, I have become ill and
I have to go to the hospital now.
But I would like you to accept this painting
as a thank you for your kindness.

Vincent Van Gogh

Biography of Vincent Van Gogh

The colors of life

Almost nobody recognized the value of Vincent Van Gogh's art during his lifetime, except for his brother Theo. Although he wasn't wealthy, Theo gave Vincent money so that he could continue to paint and he told him he was sure that one day people would love his paintings. Theo also wrote Vincent regularly. In response, Vincent sent Theo hundreds of letters describing his thoughts, his hopes for his art, and his love of painting.

One of Van Gogh's letters
to his brother Theo

Portraits

Van Gogh loved to paint people. But he was shy and had no money. So he couldn't pay or persuade people to sit as his models. He did, however, paint portraits of Joseph Roulin, the postman; Joseph's wife, Augustine; their three children; and the doctor who treated him, Dr. Gachet.

Portrait of Joseph Roulin (1889), Museum of Modern Art, New York, USA

Lullaby: Madame Augustine Roulin Rocking a Cradle (1889), Museum of Fine Arts, Boston, USA

Favorite color

For Van Gogh, yellow was the color of hope. He believed it was full of life and energy — like the sun. He created many beautiful paintings of yellow things. In these he expressed his love of life.

The yellow house

In 1888, Van Gogh moved to Arles in southeastern France. Around Arles, yellow peach flowers bloom in spring and fields of tall yellow wheat ripple like waves in the breeze in summer. Van Gogh loved Arles and invited many of his artist friends to work there too. In Arles he painted many of his most famous and popular paintings.

Sunflowers (1888), National Gallery, London, UK

The Yellow House (1888), Van Gogh Museum, Amsterdam, the Netherlands

1853
Born on March 30 in the Netherlands; his father is a church minister

1857
Vincent's brother Theo is born on May 1

1869
Starts to work for an art dealer in The Hague

1878
Decides to become a minister and starts studying religion

1880
Gives up working for the church and starts studying art in Brussels

1886
Moves to Paris to live with Theo

1888
Leaves Paris and settles in Arles in southeastern France

1889
After suffering from depression, moves to a psychiatric hospital in Saint-Rémy

1890
Moves to another hospital in Auvers-sur-Oise near Paris; commits suicide on July 27

Van Gogh's despair

Self-portrait with Bandaged Ear and Pipe (1889), private collection

Soon after he moved into the yellow house in Arles, Van Gogh heard that his friend Paul Gauguin was looking for somewhere to stay. So Van Gogh invited him to Arles. Though he had little money, he set aside a room for Gauguin and bought new furniture for it.

Van Gogh wanted to work side by side with Gauguin. But this wasn't easy, as both artists were sensitive and had strong opinions. They began to argue all the time and one day Gauguin packed up and left. Van Gogh was so frustrated and sad that he cut off his own earlobe with a razor. Afterwards, he painted himself and showed his sadness and pain.

Self-portrait (1889), Musée d'Orsay, Paris, France

Expressions of loneliness

Van Gogh became more and more unhappy. As a result he was admitted to a psychiatric hospital in Saint-Rémy near Arles. His room at the hospital had just one small window with iron bars. Van Gogh started painting the scenes he could see through this window. One of his most famous works from this time is *The Starry Night*. Clearly the stars looked very bright and beautiful to Van Gogh. Another work, *Sorrowing Old Man*, expresses his loneliness at the hospital.

The Starry Night (1890), Museum of Modern Art, New York, USA

Sorrowing Old Man (At Eternity's Gate) (1890),
Kröller-Müller Museum, Otterlo, the Netherlands

Although he received treatment, Van Gogh became sadder and lonelier. In the summer of 1890, on his brother's advice, he moved to another hospital in Auvers-sur-Oise, near Paris. But this didn't make him feel any better. On July 27, he shot himself. He is buried in the church cemetery at Auvers-sur-Oise.

Van Gogh sold very few paintings in his lifetime and achieved little success. He ended his life sad and disappointed. But today his paintings are immensely popular, and their bright colors make many people happy. Today Van Gogh is much loved – and his brother Theo is remembered fondly too.

"They said he was crazy,

but they didn't really know him.

I discovered he was a gentle soul

with a pure and beautiful heart."